Personal Growth

Reaching Your True Potential And Making A Plan For Your Own Personal Journey To Success And Enlightenment

By Ace McCloud
Copyright © 2014

Disclaimer

The information provided in this book is designed to provide helpful information on the subjects discussed. This book is not meant to be used, nor should it be used, to diagnose or treat any medical condition. For diagnosis or treatment of any medical problem, consult your own physician. The publisher and author are not responsible for any specific health or allergy needs that may require medical supervision and are not liable for any damages or negative consequences from any treatment, action, application or preparation, to any person reading or following the information in this book. Any references included are provided for informational purposes only. Readers should be aware that any websites or links listed in this book may change.

Table of Contents

Introduction 6
Chapter 1: The Attitude of Personal Growth 8
Chapter 2: Personal Growth Strategies 9
Chapter 3: Your Own Personal Growth Journey 16
Chapter 4: Personal Growth Resources 21
Chapter 5: Role Models of Personal Growth 24
Conclusion 26
My Other Books and Audio Books 27

Be sure to check out my website for all my Books and Audio books.

www.AcesEbooks.com

Introduction

I want to thank you and congratulate you for buying the book, "Personal Growth: Reaching Your True Potential And Making A Plan For Your Own Personal Journey To Success and Enlightenment."

Do you often find yourself wishing you that you could get more out of your life? As you move from childhood to adulthood, you grow in many ways, physically and mentally. Still, you may often find yourself having to go the extra mile to give yourself the "push" needed to obtain success and happiness. Your life is only what you make of it. To set yourself up for the best life possible, you must make a conscious decision to step up, in order to step forward.

Personal growth has many definitions, but what does it mean to you? In general, it means that there is always room for improvement in your life. On personal terms, it means that you can always find a way to improve an area of your life. Whether you are looking to improve your career skills to make more money, your exercise skills to get in better shape, your money handling skills to improve your finances, your personal development skills so you can be the best you can possibly be, or any other area of your life, this book can help you!

Think about your life for one second. Do you feel that you possess more negative traits than positive? If so, it is not your fault, and you can reverse them entirely. People tend to pick up on negative traits from negative people. To begin your personal growth journey and to get rid of those negative traits forever, you must be aware of positive traits. Think about the people in your life who are happy, successful, and fulfilled. You, too, can be like that.

This book contains proven steps and strategies on how to set yourself up for success on your very own personal growth journey. You will discover how to get started by reading about some of the best strategies to practice for self-development. You will also learn how to map out your own, customized journey so that you can take yourself ahead in life. To help you, you will also gain access to some very helpful personal growth resources and you will read about some role models in the personal growth field. What are you waiting for? Read on and learn how to make some incredible changes that will aid you on your personal journey through life!

Chapter 1: The Attitude of Personal Growth

When you make a conscious decision to work towards improving your life and the lives of others, you are making a decision to develop yourself—also known as engaging in personal growth. Many people undergo some sort of self-development as they go through school, work at different jobs, and live through different experiences. However, everybody's lives are different and not everybody will feel fulfillment at the same pace. If you're not satisfied with your job, your health, your spirituality, or your general happiness, you may need to further your level of personal growth to gain a better quality of life.

Personal growth does not happen overnight. In fact, it takes a little effort each day to improve. First, you must know which areas of your life you would like to focus on. However, this can take time. The more you learn, the more you explore, and the more you apply your strengths and talents, the more you can develop yourself until you're happy. Tony Robbins, a well-known life coach and author, defined it this way: "Constant and never-ending improvement (CANI)." No matter how old you are or how much education you've received, anyone can partake in a personal growth journey with just a bit of commitment each day.

Experiencing personal growth can be very refreshing. It can help you increase your chances of earning more money in life; it can turn you from a follower into a leader, and it can help you achieve self-awareness. It can dramatically improve your life's quality, as you can explore new hobbies, learn new things, and maximize your social skills. Personal growth can push you to be in the best health, physically and mentally. It can make you look more appealing to potential employers, and it can help you strive to be the best you can be overall. The possibilities are endless when it comes to personal growth. You can always find something to learn or improve. When you notice or feel a change in your life—a positive one—you have successfully experienced personal growth.

Personal growth has been a topic that has been studied for many years. Abraham Maslow, a psychologist, famously included the principle at the top of his Hierarchy of Needs. Today, working on your personal growth is essential for living a happy, fulfilling, and successful life. Again, developing yourself will not happen overnight and you will need to commit to working hard towards your goals.

Imagine living the life you want—well, stop imagining, because you can! It probably won't be easy… it never is, but if you have the [desire](#) and [motivation](#) to succeed, nearly anything is possible!

Chapter 2: Personal Growth Strategies

To get your personal growth journey jump-started, you will need to have some strategies in mind. To see changes, you must take action, and to take action, you will need to test out some of these strategies. Luckily, most of the best personal growth strategies are easy to implement in your daily life. Some of them also serve as advice, so it is a good idea to read through the whole list. The ones that are most important to you will stick with you. You will read about many strategies, so do not become overwhelmed. Pick a few that are appealing to you, start slow, and then gradually work your way through others. Your goal is to take the most important strategies that work well for you and change them into a habit that you do every day.

The Best Personal Growth Strategies

Set Goals. First and foremost, you must set goals in order to experience any kind of personal growth. While you shouldn't obsess over your future, it is a good idea to have a rough plan of where you are and where you want to be. You can set short-term and long-term goals. Sometimes, a good strategy is to set short-term goals to work toward a long-term goal. Your goals can serve as your road maps to your life, so set them well! Without setting goals, it is likely that you will not make any progress toward the new you. A good strategy is to start a goal out with the phrase: "I will easily…" For example, if your goal is to be nicer to people, your goal could be something like: "I will easily be friendlier and nicer to people and smile often." Once your goals have been made, try and choose a date by which the goal will be achieved, and be sure to read through your goals daily and while you are doing this, think about "WHY" you want to accomplish this goal so badly!

Stay Present. To make the most of your life, you should focus on your present self and not your past or future self. What you do in the present moment can have a direct impact your future. You should still plan for the future, of course, by setting goals that you work towards in the present moment. Do not worry about the past; leave it where it is. Your past is what brought you to the present, so live the present well to get to your next destination. Forgiveness is a huge part of this. Life is so much better when you don't think about the past, don't worry about the future, and just live in the present. Some great resources that can help you with this is Mindfulness Meditation from Hypnosis Downloads, my book on Forgiveness and my favorite forgiveness and healing YouTube video of all time: Tapping into Forgiveness with Brad Yates. These are things that you want to do at least once a day, and probably twice a day for a month to truly see some incredible results. If your find your thoughts overcome with worry and Fear, be sure to check out my bestselling book: Overcome Fear.

Ignore Negative Opinions. Do not let the thoughts of other people distract you from your goals or your journey. Although it may be hard, remind yourself that it is your job to make yourself happy, not others. As long as you are happy with your decisions and where they take you, your independent will can grow strong and durable. Ignoring the opinions of others is not an emergency situation—people often get over it and they even tend to respect you for staying true to yourself. This is especially important, and if there are people who are constantly trying to bring you down or hinder your success, it may be time to think about alienating them from your life and finding some more supportive people to hang out with.

Focus Deep. Instead of trying to experience everything by scratching surfaces, try to pick a few things on which you want to focus and on which you want to develop. For example, if you're a student with an engineering major, pick a subcategory of engineering into which you really want to dig and focus on. Don't try to cram your all into every single engineering class that your school offers. Staying focused and narrow on one or two things can help you develop an expertise, which can help you in both your life and your career. It is also critical in every day endeavors. By focusing your full attention on one task, going deep and hard into the subject matter, and finishing it to the best of your ability, you will find that not only will you be able to get much more done, but you will also be seeing much more quality results as well. Group similar tasks together and then getting it all done as quickly and as focused as possible is also another way to be much more productive.

Make Mistakes. One of the facts of life is that nobody is perfect and you will more than likely fail at something at some point. Instead of letting it discourage you, use failure to your advantage. You can use it to re-evaluate yourself and figure out where you can improve for next time. In some cases, you may realize that failing at one thing can bring you to something better. If you never fail, you will never learn from experience. The key is never to repeat the same failure. If you want to avoid making mistakes in the first place, a great idea is to model yourself after someone successful in the area you are trying to thrive in, and take advice and lessons from them.

Don't Victimize Yourself. If you victimize yourself or otherwise let yourself become stressed out over minor situations, start working to change this. Struggling against factors that you cannot change can be mentally draining and can hold you back from moving towards better things in your life. Studies have shown that optimistic people are more successful in life than pessimistic people.

Have Values. When you have established values in your life, your decisions tend to be a reflection of, or a step toward those values. Common core values include religion, having good morals, believing in family, and taking care of your health. Your values can help guide you through your journey, so choose them well! If you are a business owner, make sure that your company has values, as well. As most everyone knows, In life and in business, your reputation is everything.

Be Open to New Experiences. The beauty of life is that you are never too old to learn something new. Even if you have been out of school for years, you can always learn something new. Experiencing new things can help you become more aware of your strengths and talents and it can make you a more interesting person. You can learn in many ways —read a book, read the news, get a part-time job, travel, etc. The possibilities are endless!

Pay Kindness Forward. It seems that kindness to strangers has become a rarity in our world today. By exerting kindness to others: holding doors for each other, offering help, or even by simply smiling at somebody, you can potentially make a change in another person's life. Though it may not seem like it on the surface, paying kindness forward can actually affect (positively) hundreds of lives. Also, knowing that you've done something nice for another person feels great!

Volunteer. Volunteering can help you give back to others and is another way to pay some kindness forward, especially around the holidays. It's also a great way to get out of the house and expand your social network. You never know what opportunities can come out of volunteering for a good cause. You will feel great about yourself knowing that you could lend a helping hand to someone or a family in need. Volunteer work also looks great on a resume.

Count Your Blessings. When you're young, it may seem easy to take some of the most important things for granted -- your family, the roof over your head, the clothes you're wearing, etc. As you get older, you will likely gain a better sense of just how hard you have to work to keep those things. If you want to feel good and maintain positive thoughts, counting your blessings is a good activity. Even if you find yourself in dark times, always think about the good things that you have in your life—things that someone else may not have. This is something I will do whenever I am not feeling that great, and it always is a good pick up. Another common term for counting your blessings is just all the things that you are grateful for in your life.

Read. Reading is an excellent way to learn and best of all, you can do it anywhere—at home, in nature, in a coffee shop, or anywhere else that you feel most comfortable. You're already reading this book, so congratulations, because it shows that you are looking to start or supplement your personal growth journey. For the most personal growth, I highly recommend reading selectively— look out for the best reviewed books that are aimed toward specific areas upon which you want to improve. Don't just read, either—take notes, use markers, etc. Of course, don't forget to relax with a good fiction book from time to time! If a certain book really rings true for you, be sure to save it and read it from time to time. Your motivation and desire require constant upkeep to keep that fire going!

Learn Online. Many free classes are offered online that you can take to broaden your horizons and help supplement your personal growth. Even though most free online courses do not come with any credentials upon completion, your biggest gain will be knowledge. Most online classes that cost money give you a certificate or degree at the end, which you can use to further your career. Also, many colleges now offer online and hybrid classes. There are also a variety of personal growth courses you can purchase, my favorite being Get The Edge from Tony Robbins.

Exercise Your Brain. Exercising your brain is a great way to stay sharp and to increase your thirst for knowledge. One good way to do this is to take a shot at the daily Sudoku puzzle or crossword puzzle in your daily newspaper—you don't have to sit there and complete the whole thing but give it your best shot. You can even download and play games that help exercise your brain. As a former pro gamer, I will still occasionally play some video games, and I actually think it gives me a competitive edge being able to keep my mind and reflexes sharp.

Travel. If possible, travel as much as you can. Don't pass on opportunities to travel or to see new places. By doing this, you can experience new cultures, new places, new food, and a whole different atmosphere, which can help you enhance your sense of the world. Some people even get very inspired by traveling. Travel by yourself and see if you can make it in the real world. You are bound to learn something.

Create Things. By creating things, anything from a small doodle on a piece of paper to writing an entire book, you can allow your brain to flex with all the room it needs. Are you already creative or would like to increase your creativity on a regular basis? Be sure to check out one of my personal favorite books: <u>Creativity</u>.

Reflect. Reflecting is a great strategy, for both personal and spiritual growth. By spending some time alone with yourself and thinking about your life, your values, your habits, and your goals, you can evaluate your life and then strategize to make any changes that you may need. In today's busy world, it can be easy to lose sight of your goals. Reflecting from time to time can help you stay on track.

Practice Trust. If anybody has ever let you down or disappointed you in some way, it is only natural that you have mentally built a wall around yourself for personal protection. However, if you live your life in fear, you probably will not get very far. The key is to trust your life. You were born for a reason and your life may take you on a bumpy path. View every bad experience as a lesson to be learned and trust that your life is taking you where you are meant to go. Sometimes you may have to go through three or more people that may not be ideal for your life, but if you keep at it, you will eventually be able to find a nice group of people who are trustworthy and supportive.

Challenge Yourself. Certain repeated actions can become second nature and while that can be a good thing, it can also keep you in the same place. A great personal growth strategy is to challenge yourself. Challenges can help you grow your strengths and talents. They require you to use your brain and solve problems. The more you solve problems and seek new information, the more value you will bring to yourself and the more ideas and good strategies you can come up with.

Exercise. Not only is exercise important for maintaining good physical health but it can also serve as a way to combat stress. Exercising can help you feel energetic and positive about yourself, which can motivate you to seek more challenges and opportunities. The better your health is, the easier it will be to improve other aspects of your life. For more advanced information on this, be sure to check out my hit books: Ultimate Health and Ultimate Energy.

Lead. To make the most of out of your life, be a leader and not a follower. Leaders tend to be able to think independently, find solutions first, and solve problems. People who are leaders tend to get the first callbacks for jobs, learn valuable inside information, get good promotions and they tend to be more satisfied in life. Followers tend to miss out on great opportunities, so definitely work on being a leader. If you would really like advanced knowledge on how to be a great leader, then be sure to check out my book on Leadership!

Develop Good Listening Skills. Knowing how to be a good listener is crucial for being more successful in your way through life. Communication is not a one-way street. Active listening can help you learn more and others will come to respect you if they know they can speak to you and you will listen earnestly. Active listening can also help you solve problems faster.

Consult Your Priorities. From time to time, be sure to ask yourself what your priorities are. Priorities change as you grow up and experience new things, so it is important to make sure that your goals are aligned with them, otherwise you may end up going in circles rather than ahead.

Make Room For Laughter. Laughter is a natural way to make yourself feel good. It can also help if you know how to laugh at yourself in some situations. Being too uptight or serious can sometimes put a damper on your soul. Remember, life is too short to be anything but happy and pleasant. Find a reason to smile every day. For a great place to learn more about laughter, please check out my book, Laughter and Humor Therapy.

Stamp Out Bad Habits. Your daily habits, no matter how small or insignificant, can have a direct impact on your goals and future. By stamping out any bad habits and getting into good habits, you can have a better chance at achieving your goals and being successful and happy. If you are not sure whether or not you have a bad habit, ask yourself if what you're doing can get you one step ahead. For more advanced knowledge on Habits, be sure to check out my bestselling book: The Top 100 Best habits.

Be a Role Model. Even if nobody is directly looking up to you, act as a role model to others, because you never know who is watching. Live up to your values and prove it through your actions. The world is full of many eyes, especially those of children, so try and always be the best that you can be and you may be surprised at the results. The more you try to make positive changes in the world; the more people will be encouraged to follow in your footsteps.

Avoid Destructive Behavior. Avoid destructive behavior like smoking, drinking, and doing drugs at all costs. These types of activities contribute very little to personal growth and will get you nowhere pleasant. Many drugs damage your brain, including your thinking and reasoning abilities, which are crucial for personal growth. Any type of destructive behavior will take you two steps backwards, even if you've made it one step forward.

Time Yourself. The more you can get done in life, whether at work or at home, the better your chances are at being successful in life. Having a quick turn-around rate on your work can increase your potential to make more money, especially if you are self-employed. Time yourself on your projects to see how far you can get within a certain time frame. Then, see what you can do to improve for the next time.

Take Advantage of a Full Day. Life is short and unexpected, so do not sleep it away. By waking up early every day, you can find time to get more done. You can wake up early to work on your personal projects, exercise, get a head start on your day's work, or whatever you need to do that you can get you one step ahead.

Keep an Agenda. By keeping an agenda, or by just simply organizing your projects in a notebook or on the computer, you can improve your focus, efficiency, and productivity. You can also write down and review your goals and ideas. Keeping your tasks and your thoughts organized can help you grow and stay on track.

Be Actionable. Instead of putting your tasks or goals off, dive straight into them. Procrastinating on anything will not get you anywhere and the more you can get done, the more experiences you can have. Going straight to work on them can increase your chances of completing them.

Think Before You Act. Get into the habit of taking a minute or two, before you make any decision, to think about it. Think about the consequences that can come out of each route you can take for every decision that you make. However, do not spend too much time thinking about your decisions. Otherwise you could miss out on opportunities.

Practice Visualization. Visualize yourself achieving your goals and dreams. Visualize yourself performing the steps that will take you towards your goal and think about what your life will be like once you've gotten there. This can help motivate you to achieve them in real life. Thinking about completing your goals can help you get excited and ready to take charge.

Find a Mentor. Find a mentor—someone who is already successful and/or who has undergone a personal growth journey. Your mentor can help you plan and think about your goals, give you feedback on your progress, and can help you get through any challenges that you may face. For learning, having somebody by your side that has been in your shoes before can be really helpful.

Overcome Fear. Fear can hold you back from some of the best opportunities. Do not let fear take control of your life. Taking risks can benefit you because you can either be successful and get one step ahead or you can fail and learn from your mistakes. You may have heard the theory that if something scares you, you should aim for it. The more you practice <u>overcoming fear</u>, the deeper your personal growth journey can go.

Negotiate. Learning to negotiate with others can help you practice and maintain your social skills and persuasion skills. It can even save you money. It is also a great way to build your independent will.

Discover Your Learning Style. Everybody learns differently. Some people like to get information through reading, while others may like to get it through seeing or hearing. Some people can read a book and jump right into a task, while others may have to put in some hands-on practice before they can master it. By knowing what kind of learning style works best for you, you can focus on learning in that way.

Chapter 3: Your Own Personal Growth Journey

Now you know some excellent personal growth strategies. To get started on your own personal growth journey, you will need some type of plan. Putting a plan in place can help you stay focused and help you eventually reach the point where you want to be in life. A plan can help you keep track of your progress and on things that you want to improve. Go ahead and grab a notebook that can serve as your personal growth journal. This chapter will guide you through setting up your personal growth journal and will assist you in taking the first step towards the new you. It will break your journey down into five specific sections so you can focus on one area at a time. You can also check out my book on Leadership to help give you more ideas as well.

Career Development

Step #1: The first section of your journal will be on your career path. To get started, write your name at the top of your paper and state where you work and what position you hold. Under that, write out your career objective. In other words, state where you ultimately want to be in terms of your career. On the next line, write out "short-term career goals," leave a few spaces, and then write "long-term career goals." In the short-term career goal section, write out the things you want to accomplish within the next 1 to 2 years—things that can help you get closer to your final goal. Structure your short-term and long-term goals around each other.

Step #2: On the next page of your career development chapter will be a section to keep progress of your skills. Make a column and list a couple of skills that you would like to acquire (try to pick ones that can help you reach your long-term goal). Make a column next to your skills list and think about *how* you can develop those skills. Write down any actions that you can take to get there. Next to that, make a column where you can write down a target date by which you will try to learn each skill. Finally, make a column where you can record the results.

Step #3: On another page, write down your own answers to these important career development questions:

-Do I need to focus on developing my talents or my character?
-Have I identified my true talents, strengths, passion(s), and career values?
-How would my career be affected if I woke up one hour earlier each day?
-If I became an expert in my field, how would my life be affected?
-What actions am I taking today to help me work toward my goals?

Special Exercise: Do you consider yourself an expert at something? Is there something in your life about which you are truly passionate? Many people prosper, financially and spiritually, when they focus on sharpening a skill they have and using it in a career they love. Take a few minutes to brainstorm and think about your strengths, talents, and hobbies. Is there something at which you excel that you could turn into your career? Are there any ways you can further your knowledge on that topic? (Hint: the answer is yes!)

Financial Development

Step #1: In a new section in your journal, make a place to write down your financial goals. Having a financial plan is important so you do not spend too much money. The more you work on yourself, the more money you can make, so you should know how to deal with your finances beforehand. The first thing you can do is write down a list of your expenses. Be sure to include rent payments, mortgage payments, insurance payments, utility bills, money that you spend on food and gas, and anything else you can think of that costs you money. Writing down your expenses can help you grasp a better picture of where your money is going versus looking at a bank statement.

Step #2: On a blank page, make a section to keep your monthly budget updated. Write down your estimated budget on each line for each month, making adjustments as needed. For example, in the winter you may have to account for a higher gas bill and in the summer you may need to account for a low gas bill but a higher electric bill. This will help give you a visual on how you should allocate your money each month.

Step #3: On another blank area of your financial goal section, write down any short-term or long-term goals you have for your finances. For example, one short-term goal could be to pay off your car so you could save an additional amount of money for the long-term. Be sure to structure your short-term goals around your long-term goals.

Step #4: Review this section often and be sure to take into account any changes, whether in your pay or your expenses. Knowing that you are on top of your finances can help reduce stress and can help you focus on working on other areas of yourself.

For more information on this subject, be sure to check out my book: <u>Money: The Top 100 Best Ways To Make And Manage Money</u>.

Health Development

Step #1: In a new section of your journal, make a spot for your health-related goals. Health is important for everybody and the healthier you are, the better off you will be in life. First, make a section to list your short-term and long-term health goals. If you are not sure where to start, getting your yearly check-up may be a good idea. Don't forget to set target dates to reach each goal.

Step #2: Next to each goal, write down some ideas on what you can do to help you reach them. For example, if you want to lose weight, you can write down that you will exercise and watch what you eat. Remember, being specific can help you increase your chances of reaching your goals.

Step #3: On a new page, draw a line down the center. Label one side, "Food" and the other side, "Exercise." Use this page and the next couple of pages to keep track of what you eat and what kind of exercise you do. You can get creative in this section of your journal, since everyone's health goals will differ. You can create a page to keep track of your weight, your blood pressure, calorie intake, or any health aspect that you think you need to improve upon.

Step #4: Here are some important questions that you can answer on a new page:

-What type of exercise would I enjoy the most/be able to best fit into my schedule? Light walking? Intense cardio? Strength training?
-Am I taking advantage of getting my annual check-ups with my doctor? What might be different in my life if I did/did not?
-How are my eating habits? Do they reflect a healthy, balanced diet? Do I have any deficiencies?
-What actions am I taking today to help me move toward my health and fitness goals?

Communication Skills Development

Step #1: On a new blank page, create a section where you can keep track of your interpersonal skills. Being able to communicate well with others is crucial in helping yourself get ahead in life. If you are shy or introverted, this may be a section on which you want to focus the most. As in the other sections, take one page and write out your short-term and long-term goals for improving your communication skills. For example, you could set a goal to become a better listener or to practice talking with others, so you can master the art of networking.

Step #2: Next, create three columns on a new page and label them "Nonverbal," "Verbal," and "Assertiveness." Those are three of the most common types of communication that you can develop throughout your personal growth journey. In each column, list the skills that you want to improve upon or to develop in each category. For example, under "Nonverbal," you could choose to focus on your posture, your eye contact, and your expressions. Next to each skill, leave room to write a few ideas on executing each skill. For example, you could practice in front of the mirror a few times before trying it out on someone else.

Step #3: Ask yourself and write down your own answers to these very important communication questions:

-With what kind of tone/attitude do I speak? Is it getting me positive results?

-Do I speak clearly, in a way that everyone can understand me? Do I overuse jargon?
-How are my listening skills? Do I really listen to what others are telling me or does it just go in one ear and out the other? How does that affect my relationships?
-Are my communication skills warm, respectful, focused, and clear? Do I present myself as credible?

Special Exercise: To put your social skills to the test, there are some things you can do to get started. For many people, it is hard to talk to strangers or people that you don't know very well. After you've filled out this section in your journal, try to strike up a conversation with somebody unfamiliar to you and see what happens. Pay attention to each skill that you've picked to develop and see how well you can practice it. This exercise can help you get a feel for where you are in terms of comfortable communication skills, which can be helpful for when you decide to develop them further or decide to focus on another area.

Personal Pages

Step #1: In the last section of your personal growth journal, leave some room to write whatever you think could help you grow and prosper. You could use this section to write down inspirational quotes, things for which you are grateful, or just your own thoughts on your progress. Include anything that will help you stay motivated and focused in this section. You can even paste in motivating pictures or "symbols" of your progress (for example, if you were trying to lose weight, you could paste in the tag from your newest pair of jeans to show how far you've come).

Special Exercise: Is there something that you want to accomplish but the only thing that's holding you back is fear? Now is the time to jump into action. Pick something small, the scares you, and conquer it. By taking small steps as you're learning to overcome fear, you can gradually see that fear is powerless! Conquering small things can help you gain confidence. The more confidence you gain, the more likely you will be able to move on to conquering bigger fears.

If you are extra anxious about trying to conquer your fears, fill out the answers to these questions before you try:

-Is what I am doing dangerous? Is it a real danger or am I just imagining things?
-Am I mistaking danger for excitement?
-What will I do in the worst-case scenario?
-Is there anything I can do beforehand to protect myself?

This section is entirely up to you, so be creative and most importantly, have fun!

To get started, set up your journal, and then re-read Chapter 2 to get some ideas of where to begin. The next chapter will also direct you to some of the best personal growth resources that you can use as you fill out your journal.

Chapter 4: Personal Growth Resources

If you are having trouble getting a head start on your own personal growth journey, there is no need to worry, since there is an abundance of resources available to help you. I have chosen some of the best resources that I think can help anybody as they move through a personal growth journey. I have tried to include a variety of resources, since I know everyone has a different way of learning.

YouTube Videos

YouTube is a great outlet for visual learning. Everybody has a different way of learning—some people learn by reading, some learn by listening, and some learn by watching or a combination of these three. Since YouTube is a public social media channel, anyone can post personal growth-related videos. However, I have found some of the best videos that you can watch to get started:

Noah Hammond YouTube Channel

Noah Hammond is a self-proclaimed expert on personal growth and leadership. A person who underwent his own personal growth journey after a college break up, Noah Hammond aims to help people find themselves and their life purpose. On his YouTube channel, you can watch videos, personalized toward men *and* women that focus on improving health, social skills, spirituality, and anything else that you can think of in the area of personal growth. To get started, check out his video on Finding Your Life Purpose, which includes some interactive exercises for you to try as you watch.

Here are some more YouTube videos you can check out to get a better idea on personal growth:

Will Smith on Personal Growth posted by BrandNewLifeBodyByVi
Personal Growth Binaural Beats + Isochronic Tones by OspreyMusicInc
10 Steps fto Create your Professional Development Plan by Christine Scivicque
7 Great Coaching Tips To Skyrocket Your Personal Development by Thomas Di Leva

Hypnosis

Experimenting with hypnosis can help you get started on your personal growth journey. Hypnosis is a form of psychology that can help your brain get into a certain mindset. At Hypnosisdownloads.com, you can check out some great self-hypnosis resources that have been developed by experienced hypnotherapists. The ones that I would recommend the most for personal growth is the Stellar Success course, which has worked wonders for me. Also be sure to check out the Personal Growth, Personal Power, and Personal Change downloads. There are many more specific topic downloads so be sure to take advantage of the search option to find the right download for yourself. This is something I try to do every day, and I highly recommend it.

Tony Robbins, Life Coach

You may remember Tony Robbins from Chapter 1. He is a very well-known life coach who has been able to impact the lives of people all over the world. He is best known for his inspirational quotes and coaching packages and someone I have been actively following and purchasing from for the last ten years. To learn more about him, please visit his website at www.tonyrobbins.com.

Seminars, Webinars, and Workshops

By attending seminars, webinars, and workshops, you can participate in a hands-on learning experience. You also have the opportunity to meet other people who are in the same position as you. Additionally, you may meet somebody who can become your personal growth mentor. These events are often inspirational, unique, and very effective. Try to attend at least one personal development event during your journey, if possible.

The best way to find out more information on these events is to look online. You can usually learn about upcoming events on the professional networking website, LinkedIn. You can also find events, both local and state-wide, on the website SkillPath. Finally, be sure to keep your eyes peeled in your local newspapers for any upcoming personal growth events in your area. Live Your Legend is also a very popular group that may be in your local area. If you absolutely cannot travel, look around for webinars—they are the same as seminars, but you can watch them over your computer.

Helpful Products

If you do not set goals for yourself, it is very likely that you will not get far on your personal growth journey. It can be easy to set your goals in your head, but by writing them down, you can remember them better and it serves as a visual reminder. You can write your goals down on any type of paper, but for optimal results, I highly recommend checking out the 90 Day Goal Planner. This planner can help you ensure that you can move through your goals quickly and efficiently.

Also, if your body is not getting the right amount of nutrients it needs to function properly, you can become tired, run down, fatigued, or be faced with other health issues that can distract you from bettering other aspects of your life. While it will take some planning to get your health life really in order, you can start by ensuring that you get all the vitamins and minerals you need through a multivitamin. If you're not sure what brand to try, I highly recommend the Optimum Nutrition brand. It works great and offers special versions for men and women. But to truly become your best, it always comes down to health and energy. Get these mastered, and everything else tends to fall into place much easier as long as you are using proper self-discipline.

Chapter 5: Role Models of Personal Growth

Though some people may think that working through personal growth is not worth the effort, it is. People in history who have changed the world are proof. Many successful people have attributed things such as values, the quest for a life worth living, the want for a better quality of life, and personal challenges as things that have helped them become the people who were able to leave their legacies and make a true impact on the world. You, too, can improve your quality of life despite anything that has ever happened. As long as you focus on developing your personal growth and improving your life, you can do amazing things. You never know—your own personal growth journey could take you to places you'd never even dream of going. This chapter will take a look at the lives of 5 of some of the most well-known, world-changing people who overcame their own challenges by way of personal growth.

Nelson Mandela

Nelson Mandela is one of the most famous people to display the traits of personal growth. Before his death, he was an activist for South Africa who led peaceful protests in an attempt to integrate different races within the country. As a young person, he spent many years studying. Some of his protests landed him in jail for 30 years. After he was released from jail, he went on to become the president of South Africa, succeeded at his many attempts for reform, and even created a diverse government council. After his time as president, he continued to advocate for peace, both worldwide and in South Africa, despite some health issues. Nelson Mandela is a great example of a man who achieved personal growth. He never appeared discouraged, even while he was in prison, where many were treated inhumanely. Despite ongoing health issues, he continued to play a part in the world until his death. One of his most famous quotes is, "There is nothing like returning to a place that remains unchanged to find the ways in which you yourself have altered."

Helen Keller

Helen Keller is another great personal growth role model. When she was a young child, an illness rendered her blind and deaf. With the help of a teacher, she was able to learn how to read, spell, and write. She eventually got accepted into college and began a writing career. She wrote for magazines and newspapers and wrote her own autobiography. Throughout her life, she also advocated for workers and woman's rights and protested World War I. Most significantly, she developed an organization which eventually became known as Helen Keller International. Through this organization, she traveled the globe and rallied for blind people. Once, she famously said, "We could never learn to be brave and patient if there were only joy in the world," meaning that without challenges and obstacles, you would not be able to learn from your experiences and work toward bettering yourself.

Steve Jobs

As you probably know, Steve Jobs is the guy behind Apple. Most well-known for creating the iPod, Mac, iPad, and more, he actually came a long way before anybody ever knew his name. Originally an orphan, he attended college but dropped out. Sources have said that he would take various classes to gain whatever knowledge he could. The company known as Apple today began in the garage of his parents' house. Because he had a vision to change the world, Jobs went from sleeping on floors and making money by recycling glass bottles to becoming one of the most successful people in the world. Steve Jobs is an excellent example of how anyone can develop himself. He thrived on knowledge and used it to do something amazing.

Oprah Winfrey

Oprah Winfrey, a well-known talk show host and one of the richest women in the world, who had to overcome a hard life before she ever rose to the top. Raised by a single mother, she grew up in poverty and was sexually molested. By age 14, she was on her own and experienced a teenage pregnancy in which she lost the baby. Despite her hardships, she was granted a scholarship to college, where she studied communications, and worked her way up in broadcasting until she developed her own show. She began to advocate for other children who were sexually abused and she also gives money to those in need to help them improve their lives. Winfrey once said, "Do one thing you think you cannot do. Fail at it. Try again. Do better the second time. The only people who never tumble are those who mount the high wire. This is your moment. Own it."

Sam Walton

The story of Sam Walton is a great example about how exploring versatile jobs can help you with personal growth. Since he grew up in a poor family, he began doing odd jobs to help support them. His first business of sorts was to bottle, sell, and deliver milk from cows that the family owned. By taking on a job selling magazine subscriptions, he was able to practice his sales skills early on. He worked odd jobs through college until he made an investment into a general retail store which eventually grew into Walmart. The story of Sam Walton is proof that as long as you work hard and you explore different opportunities, you can set yourself up for a better future. He shows that by working hard, providing quality, and learning as much as possible, that success is inevitable. He never gave up, never stopped supporting his family, and finally struck gold.

Conclusion

I hope this book was able to help you to figure out which areas of your life that you can improve upon and how you can get started.

The next step is to use of the strategies learned from Chapter 2: and do something immediately! Even if you just write on a piece of scrap paper, write down one area of your life on which you are going to start working on and one strategy that you are going to use to do it. Start from there and work your way through the other areas of your life. Remember, don't rush through anything and don't try to do it all at once—start slow and gradually work your way into becoming a happy, successful, and fulfilled person!

Finally, if you discovered at least one thing that has helped you or that you think would be beneficial to someone else, be sure to take a few seconds to easily post a quick positive review. As an author, your positive feedback is desperately needed. Your highly valuable five star reviews are like a river of golden joy flowing through a sunny forest of mighty trees and beautiful flowers! *To do your good deed in making the world a better place by helping others with your valuable insight, just leave a nice review.*

My Other Books and Audio Books
www.AcesEbooks.com

Peak Performance Books

Health Books

Be sure to check out my audio books as well!

 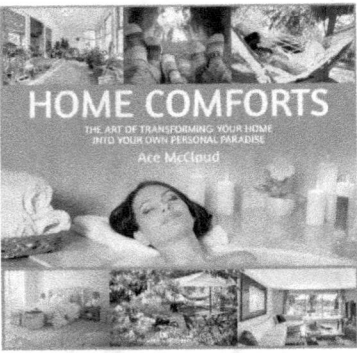 

Check out my website at: **www.AcesEbooks.com** for a complete list of all of my books and high quality audio books. I enjoy bringing you the best knowledge in the world and wish you the best in using this information to make your journey through life better and more enjoyable! **Best of luck to you!**

www.ingramcontent.com/pod-product-compliance
Lightning Source LLC
Chambersburg PA
CBHW051430070526
44584CB00023B/3667